Trillium and Toronto Island

Trillium and Toronto Island

~ The Centennial Edition ~

MIKE FILEY

DUNDURN PRESS
TORONTO

Editor: Jennifer McKnight
Design: Jennifer Scott
Printer: Marquis

Library and Archives Canada Cataloguing in Publication

Filey, Mike, 1941-
    Trillium and Toronto Island : the centennial edition / by Mike Filey. -- 3rd ed.

Includes index.
ISBN 978-1-55488-737-8

        1. Trillium (Ferry)--History. 2. Toronto Islands (Ont.)--History.
3. Toronto (Ont.)--History. I. Title.

HE5785.T6F54 2010   386'.609713541   C2009-907468-0

1   2   3   4   5   14   13   12   11   10

We acknowledge the support of the **Canada Council for the Arts** and the
Ontario Arts Council for our publishing program. We also acknowledge the
financial support of the **Government of Canada** through the **Canada Book
Fund** and **The Association for the Export of Canadian Books**, and the
Government of Ontario through the **Ontario Book Publishers Tax Credit
program**, and the **Ontario Media Development Corporation**.

Care has been taken to trace the ownership of copyright material used in this book.
The author and the publisher welcome any information enabling them to rectify
any references or credits in subsequent editions.

                                        J. Kirk Howard, President

Printed and bound in Canada.
www.dundurn.com

Dundurn Press
3 Church Street, Suite 500
Toronto, Ontario, Canada
M5E 1M2

Gazelle Book Services Limited
White Cross Mills
High Town, Lancaster, England
LA1 4XS

Dundurn Press
2250 Military Road
Tonawanda, NY
U.S.A. 14150

Dedicated to all those who worked on this remarkable project
and to those who keep *Trillium* shipshape.

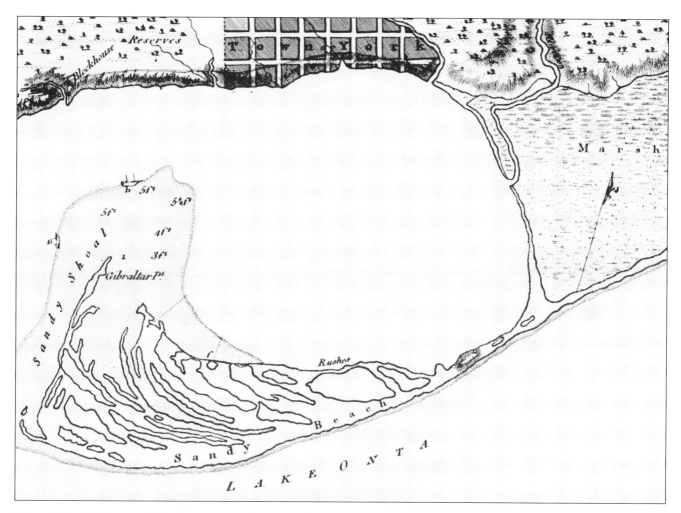

Plan of York (Toronto) Harbour, 1815, by Joseph Bouchette (1774–1841).
"I found [York Harbour] to be without comparison the most proper situation for an arsenal in every extent
of that word that can be met with in this province. The spit of sand which forms its entrance is capable
of being so fortified with a few heavy guns as to prevent any vessel from entering the harbour, or from
remaining within it."

Contents

Foreword to the Original Edition

There are times when politicians show remarkable foresight for what seems very little immediate political gain. I think of the City fathers in the early years of this century who constructed the Prince Edward Viaduct over Bloor Street cutting a passage for a subway line which was finally needed some fifty years later.

This is the kind of foresight which will bring praise to the members of Metro Toronto Council, who in November 1973 voted to restore the ferry boat *Trillium*. Not, this time, to provide for an unknown future, but to preserve the known past.

Preservation of the *Trillium* has been a popular undertaking. Much attention to its restoration was given by the public and the media. But it was not the kind of project for which citizens were collecting petitions or banging on the doors of City Hall to demand action. It took some foresight and some courage on the part of some politicians to put up the necessary one million dollars.

I became involved in and enthusiastic about the restoration of *Trillium* at an early stage, when it was still a near wreck located in a lagoon at the Toronto Islands. The Toronto Historical Board, and in particular Mike Filey, approached me about the idea of saving the vessel and I in turn helped them to convince Parks Commissioner Tommy Thompson and Metro Council that the project was worthwhile.

What persuaded them to approve this project? It's difficult to pin down. The report of marine engineering consultant Gordon Champion indicated that the hull and some engine parts were in good shape (the superstructure would have to be replaced) and that building a new ferry boat would cost several times the amount required to restore *Trillium* — although nobody suggested that a new ferry was needed anyway. For me, and some others, a key factor in reaching a favourable decision was *Trillium*'s link with Toronto's past and the enjoyment that future generations would have riding on this 1910 side-paddle wheeler — a piece of living history now proudly returned to service.

Arthur C. Eggleton
Mayor of Toronto 1980–1991
MP for York Centre 1993–2004
Appointed Senator for Ontario March 24, 2005

Preface to the Centennial Edition

This book, which was first published in 1976, the year the restored *Trillium* returned to take its place as the Queen of the Toronto Island ferry boat fleet, has been long out of print. However, as the 100th anniversary of the launching of *Trillium* at the Polson ship yard on Toronto's eastern waterfront approached I found myself eager to reprint the book. In addition to incorporating a selection of photographs that came to light after the initial printing I have also added other photos that show this historic vessel in a much different Toronto following the million dollar restoration.

Since the first edition of the book was done without the use of a computer it was necessary to re-key all the text and captions and this was quickly and capably done by my wife Yarmila. Thank you, again. Additional historic photos, some from the City of Toronto Archives or Toronto Transit Commission Archives and many others were discovered thanks to searches on the incredible internet. A few modern-day views were supplied by Torontonian Phillip Troyer and Andy Burgess, the latter gentleman being a visitor from England who happened to be touring the city's waterfront when he snapped the photo of *Trillium* and *Empire Sandy*. This unique view was subsequently posted on the internet by spacing.ca and I was able to trace its origin thanks to staff at *Spacing* magazine.

Others who have been helpful in the ongoing success of *Trillium* as both an operating vessel and unique tourist attraction include James Dann, Gary Sims, Charles Colenutt, Captain Tony Cole, Tony Heasmith, and Victor Pavlenko.

My thanks as well to Kirk Howard and his staff at the Dundurn Group, in particular Jennifer McKnight, who helped stick-handle the book through the process.

And, of course, another big thank you to my wife Yarmila who, in addition to typing the original manuscript in the days before word processing was popular, also retyped the text from the only copy I had of the original edition that first appeared 34 years ago.

Preface to the Original Edition

It was the year 1910. On May 6, Toronto's 342,000 citizens learned of the death of King Edward and the ascension to the throne of his popular son George, Duke of York. Later that same month Torontonians were supplied for the first time with chlorinated water. Out at Trethewey Farm, eight miles northwest of the city, Count Jacques de Lesseps was giving a demonstration of his flying skills. Signs of progress were in the air.

Buried on the back pages of the local dailies that June was a brief mention of the launching of a new steam ferry for the Toronto Ferry Company. Christened *Trillium*, this double-end, side-paddle Island ferry cruised the waters of Toronto Bay for nearly fifty years. Retired in 1956, the historic old craft was saved from the scrap yard when a rescue plan proposed in 1973 culminated in her return to Toronto in 1976 as a fully operational steam ferry.

The following pages trace the history of passenger travel to Toronto Island, early life on the Island, and the rise, fall, and rebirth of the most popular Island ferry boat of all, the *Trillium*.

Acknowledgements to the Original Edition

Although most of the photographs in this book are from my personal collection, I am indebted to the following agencies and people for the loan of additional photos and research facilities: City of Toronto Archives; Metro Toronto Public Library and the John Ross Robertson Collection; Hospital for Sick Children Archives; Toronto Transit Commission Archives; Toronto Harbour Commission Archives; Edith Firth; Scott James; John Jursa; Ken Rowe; Margaret Van Every; John D. Thompson; Larry Becker; Ted Wickson; and Robert Campbell. If I have omitted anyone despite my careful efforts to identify all photo sources, I apologize.

The interest of three people, Art Eggleton, Tommy Thompson, and Alan Howard, made the success of the *Trillium* project a certainty from the beginning. To them — thanks. I would like to thank Gordon Champion for technical assistance in the preparation of this book and more importantly for a job extremely well done as the Project Engineer. I also appreciate the help of those at PMA who worked on the production of this book: Kathy, Carol, Diana, Valerie, Blain, and Peter.

A special thank you is due to my Yarmila, who after quietly suffering through endless hours of meetings, discussions, and photographic sessions, typed the manuscript and offered constructive criticism.

Early History of
Toronto Island

Town of York as seen from Gibraltar Point on the peninsula, 1828. Gibraltar Point was named by Governor Simcoe because of its military resemblance to Gibraltar on the Mediterranean Sea. Note the steamboat on the bay, typical of the craft that followed Canada's first steam vessel, *Frontenac*.

In the beginning it wasn't an island. In fact, it wasn't much more than a pile of sand resting at the bottom of what we now know as Lake Ontario. About ten thousand years ago most of present-day Toronto south of St. Clair Avenue was covered by the waters of Lake Iroquois. This body of water flooded the southern part of the city towards the end of the Pleistocene age. Slowly, ever so slowly, the water of this prehistoric lake receded until by 6000 B.C. the familiar outline of Lake Ontario took shape. About this time, a thin strip of beach emerged above the water's surface. The ribbon of sand was connected to the mainland at the east end and wound its way westerly, terminating in a hooked promontory opposite the foot of what is now Bathurst Street.

Geologists tell us that this pile of sand resulted from the constant erosion of the bluffs in Scarborough. Carried west by the strong Niagara current, the sand was deposited off shore of the wooded acreage which is now Toronto. This action continued for hundreds of years, piling sand on top of sand, until a substantial peninsula was formed. The prevailing west winds and surface currents tore at the sandy ridge preventing its further growth to the west. Thus the hook was formed.

Soon vines and ferns, poplars and pines began to appear, and during the years 1755–59, the French explorer Pouchot described the north shore of Lake Ontario as follows:

> At the beginning of the Grand Ecors (Scarborough Heights), there appears the mouth of a considerable river. These Ecors are banks … eighty or ninety feet high and continue for five leagues. At the end of this distance is a point of land, wooded and forming a peninsula and in the rear a large bay partly covered with rushes.

In a map prepared by La Broquerie in October 1757, the peninsula is plainly visible. La Broquerie called it "Prè ille de Toronto." Nothing much is heard of the peninsula over the ensuing thirty or so years until this entry appears in Elizabeth Simcoe's diary for Sunday, August 4, 1793, five days after she arrived at the site of her husband's new capital of Upper Canada:

> We rode on the peninsula opposite Toronto, so I called the spit of land, for it is united to the mainland by a very narrow neck of ground. We crossed the bay opposite the camp and rode by the lake side to the end of the peninsula. We met with good natural meadows and several ponds. The trees are mostly of the poplar kind, covered with wild vines, and there are some fir. On the ground were everlasting peas creeping in abundance, of a purple colour. I am told they are good to eat when boiled, and some pretty white flowers like lily of the valley. We continued our ride beyond the peninsula on the sands of the north shore of Lake Ontario till we were impeded by large trees on the beach…. The variety of scenes I met with this morning made the ride

extremely pleasant. The wooded part
of the peninsula was like a shrubbery.
The sands towards the lake reminded
me of the sands at Weymouth.

The following Saturday, Elizabeth again confided
in her diary:

I went to my favourite sands; the bay
is a mile across. The Governor thinks,
from the manner in which the sand-
bars are formed, they are capable of
being fortified so as to be impreg-
nable; he therefore calls it 'Gibraltar
Point,' though the land is low.

During her short stay in the new capital, Elizabeth
Simcoe wrote frequently of her outings to her "favourite sands," as she called the peninsula. As well as the
attraction of its natural beauty, the peninsula had special medicinal powers as described in the *Provincial
Gazetteer* of 1799: "the long beach or peninsula,
which affords a most delightful ride, is considered so
healthy by the Indians, that they resort to it whenever
indisposed." The publication went on to describe
how beneficial the new bridge over the Don River
would be when completed, affording easy access for
the populace to the peninsula and its pleasures.

Again there is a gap in references to the peninsula,
until October 5, 1833, when the *Courier* of Upper
Canada carried the following advertisement:

The Retreat on the Peninsula

Michael O'Connor, formerly stew-
ard of the steam packet *Canada*, begs
leave respectfully to announce to the
inhabitants of York and to strangers
visiting the capital of Upper Canada
that he has opened a Hotel on the
Peninsula, opposite the Town, where
he will be ready to accommodate
Sportsmen, parties of pleasure, and
individuals who may wish to inhale
the Lake breeze.

In order to attract customers to his hotel,
O'Connor established the first public ferry service
across the bay. He emphasized the advantages of this
mode of transportation by appending to his ad:

N.B. As the proprietor has established
a Horse Boat to run regularly between
York and this place, ladies and gentlemen can make certain of returning to
suit their own convenience.

Week Days

Leaves York	Leaves Peninsula
10 morning	11 morning
2 afternoon	3 afternoon
4 afternoon	6 afternoon

On Sundays

The Boat will leave York, at 8 o'clock every morning and return at 9. Starts again at 1 o'clock p.m. and continues running the remainder of the day stopping at each side.

Passage to and from the Peninsula, 7 ½ d.
Children half price.
Season tickets can be had on board the Boat.

York, Oct. 2, 1833.

Shortly after O'Connor established his hotel on the peninsula, Benjamin Knott built a starch and soap factory nearby, moving there from his original location at the foot of Sherbourne Street on the mainland. It would appear that Knott acquired O'Connor's hotel and two-horse team boat in 1834 and placed the following advertisement in *Walton's York Commercial Directory*, 1833–34:

On the Island or Peninsula, Mr. Knott has lately erected a manufactory for making starch, soap, etc., attached to which is a hotel for the accommodation of parties of pleasure visiting the Island, and for whose convenience for getting there a boat has been established, propelled by four horses.

Elsewhere in the directory another ad reads:

A boat propelled by four horses called the Sir John of the Peninsula, runs every day from the Steam Boat Wharfs to the starch factory on the Peninsula or Island across the Bay; her trips regulated to suit public convenience.

Fare to and from the Island is 3d.

Note that even though the strip of land was still physically a peninsula, residents had begun referring to it as an island. A year later, in 1835, the hotel again changed hands and was operated as the Peninsula Hotel by Messrs. Anderton and Palin. Their flowery ad in the *Upper Canada Land, Mercantile, and General Advertiser* of February 21, 1835, advised the citizens that they, Anderton and Palin, had leased the hotel with a view to "forming a pleasant and health retreat for individuals and families desirous of changing the air of the City for the salubrious atmosphere of the Island. Neat and comfortable furniture, with larder stocked with game, etc., in season, and choice wines with prompt attention will at all times be proffered."

With this new business venture came a new method of crossing the bay, new for Torontonians anyway. Forty-five years earlier, on July 26, 1790, John Fitch had operated the first steamboat operation anywhere, between Philadelphia and nearby towns on the Delaware River. In 1807, Robert Fulton began running his famous *Clermont* on the Hudson between New York and Albany, thereby establishing the first commercially successful steamboat operation in the world. Both these ventures, however, postdated the first practical steamboat, the 138-foot-long paddle wheeler *Pyroschaphe*, which was operated from Lyon to the Isle Barbe on the River Saone on July 15, 1783. Closer to home, the first steamboat to be built and to operate on the Great Lakes was launched on September 7, 1816, at Bath, near Kingston, Ontario. Steam power arrived on Toronto Bay in 1835 when Anderton and Palin replaced the houseboat with Toronto's first *steam* ferry boat, appropriately named the *Toronto*. This vessel measured sixty-two feet in length and had a thirteen-foot beam. It was propelled by a fourteen horsepower engine and was described in the *Patriot*, October 9, 1835, as "composed of the best seasoned materials, having a commodious deck cabin with fittings, and in every respect adapted for the comfort and accommodation of passengers." For some reason the vessel was removed from service and auctioned that same year. The houseboat was reinstated.

Things were busy in the Peninsula Hotel and the government completed the bridges over the mouths of the Big and Small Don River, where they emptied into the harbour. Access to the peninsula was now much easier and Palin appealed to the citizenry in an ad in the *Courier*, July 9, 1835, to use the new structures and visit the peninsula as it was "one of the most inviting and healthy rides near the city." The ad also informed the public that the hotel was fitted out with "warm and cold baths for ladies and gentlemen on the newest principle so strongly recommended by the medical profession for health and recreation."

Recognizing a good thing, the city fathers established a toll gate on the road to the peninsula in 1836.

The charges were sixpence for every four-wheeled pleasure carriage drawn by two or more horses, four pence for every other carriage or wagon drawn by two or more horses, three pence for every one horse carriage, wagon, or cart, and for every saddle horse, two pence.

With the completion of rudimentary bridges over the Don and inauguration of public ferry service to the peninsula, the quiet isolation of Mrs. Simcoe's "favourite sands" was coming to an end.

An outbreak of the dreaded cholera wreaked havoc among the fourteen thousand inhabitants of the young city of Toronto during the 1830s. One of her wealthy citizens, Charles Poulett Thompson, who was to become Lord Sydenham, governor of the United Canadas, chose to acquire Palin's Hotel on the peninsula as a summer residence away from the misery spawned by the epidemic. In 1843, Louis Privat leased the structure from the Thompson estate. As business increased a larger ferry boat became necessary. Louis and his brother Peter brought a small steamboat from the Niagara River to Toronto, converted it to a houseboat powered by two horses walking a circular treadmill, and began conveying the public to Louis's hotel on the peninsula aboard the *Peninsula Packet*, as the houseboat was called. In 1845, the vessel was enlarged and three more horsepower added. The Privats developed a small amusement park beside their hotel consisting of a merry-go-round, swings, a bowling alley, and a zoo. An advertisement in the *British Colonist* described the resort thus:

That safe and convenient houseboat, the *Peninsula Packet* will leave Mr. Maitland's Wharf, foot of Church Street, every day at 10 o'clock a.m., 12, 2, 4 and 6 p.m. for the Peninsula Hotel. Returning at 11 a.m., 1, 3, 5 and 7 p.m. precisely. Fares to and from 7½d. Family Season Tickets 4S each. Swings and merry-go-rounds, etc., for the amusement of children. Dinners, lunches, teas, etc., to be had at the shortest notice. Good pasture for horses and other cattle which can be conveyed over by the first boat — not later.

The final sentence reveals the pastoral nature of the Island in 1850.

Steam power was becoming more and more evident on the Great Lakes. It had been almost thirty-five years since the first steamboat *Frontenac* had slid down the ways at Bath, Ontario, and just fifteen years since the first steam ferry had been introduced on Toronto Bay. Now in 1850, James Good, whose foundry was located at the corner of Yonge and Queen Streets and who was to build Ontario's first railway locomotive three years later, was busily completing a new steam ferry for Mr. Privat. Named the *Victoria*, it was powered by a twenty-five horsepower steam engine and was to run from Maitland's Church Street wharf every hour on the hour between 10 a.m. and 7 p.m. during the summer season. Appended to a small ad about the *Victoria*'s operating times is a short note that it had "no connection with any other boat

or racing." This refers to the fact that at this time a crude racecourse had been laid out on the peninsula at a place called "The Bend," which was located just east of the narrow beach that connected the peninsula with the mainland.

In 1853, the old hotel came under new management for the sixth time when John Quinn acquired the business from the Privats. Quinn almost immediately introduced a companion steam ferry for the *Victoria*, which was called the *Citizen*. These two vessels enabled passengers to depart for the peninsula every thirty minutes rather than hourly as before. In the following year, 1854, a Captain Robert Moodie introduced competition on the bay when he inaugurated service with his steam ferry, the *Bob Moodie*. Moodie ran an ad in the local newspaper boasting that his new pleasure steamer could make "four trips to the Island within the hour — and speed is certainly a desideratum on that pleasure trip, the advantage of which cannot be overlooked." Moodie also made the point that "in case a gale should arise, passengers by the other line [Quinn's] need not expect to return in this boat as Captain Moodie will on such occasions only carry his own passengers." Not to be outdone, Quinn introduced his third vessel, the *Welland*, running from the Church Street wharf every twenty minutes between one and three-thirty in the afternoon and, in the manner of a modern day public relations salesman, advised the public that "those travelling by Quinn's boats may expect to receive from him that kindness which he has always shown to passengers to the Island." And almost as an afterthought, perhaps remembering all those souls left over on the peninsula, he added, "Parties remaining

Privat's Hotel on the peninsula, circa 1850.
Originally owned by Michael O'Connor and later
by Lord Sydenham, the Privat brothers acquired
the property in 1843–44. They provided guests with
amusements such as a bowling alley, zoo, and rides.
The structure was purchased later by John Quinn
and was washed away in a fierce storm in 1858.

after half past three may return by my other vessel, the steamer *Citizen*." The fever of competition seemed to have calmed, for in 1857 season tickets for either Quinn's or Moodie's vessels were interchangeable. In that same year Moodie introduced the *Lady Head*, making a total of five steam ferries — *Victoria*, *Citizen*, *Welland*, *Bob Moodie*, and *Lady Head* — running from Toronto to the peninsula.

As the reader has probably noticed, the terms *peninsula* and *island* have been used interchangeably in the advertisements quoted from the local papers. This ambivalence was probably due to the fact that the peninsula was connected to the mainland only by a narrow neck of beach which on several occasions during periods of high water was washed away. Fierce storms in 1852 and 1853 had in fact inundated this beach strip, isolating the Island from the mainland. On both occasions the gap filled with sand and silt again forming a peninsula. However, a permanent breach was made on April 13, 1858, during a particularly vicious storm. The full impact of the storm is best described in this item in the *Leader* newspaper on April 14:

> Between four and five o'clock yesterday morning, the waters of the lake completely swept over a large section of the Island, entirely carrying away Quinn's Hotel and its appurtenances, along with the excuse for a breakwater, erected by the Harbour Commissioners, and making a permanent Eastern Entrance to the Harbour, some 500 yards wide. The gale which led up to the partial washing away of the Island sprung up about five o'clock on Monday evening and was then of such violence as to cause serious fears that the hotel would be blown down. The lake gained steadily on the Island and the Hotel until about four o'clock in the morning when the Hotel was completely swept away and a very wide entrance to our harbour — some four or five feet deep — was opened through the Island. In anticipation of such an event, Mr. Quinn erected a small building west of the Hotel into which he barely had time to move his family, and a small portion of his furniture before his former residence was borne away by the waves. He is said to be a heavy loser.

Soon after the breach had been made, lake vessels including the *Eliza* and the *Highland Chief* began using the new eastern gap as a means of access to and egress from Toronto Harbour. The two schooners mentioned passed through the gap on May 31, 1858, being the first vessels to navigate the new waterway.

With the loss of Quinn's Hotel, only two permanent structures were left on Toronto Island. They were Gibraltar Point Lighthouse, the construction of which had been recommended by Governor Simcoe in 1793 but not carried out until 1809, and just to the northwest of the lighthouse the lightkeeper's shack, the first dwelling erected on the peninsula and later used as a schoolhouse until the first Island School was built in 1888. Also lost in the storm that created the eastern gap was a smaller hotel known as Parkinson's which had been erected about 1850. Following the storm, Mrs. Parkinson erected a second hotel near the present Centre Island ferry docks. In 1873, this hotel was purchased by Robert Mead, and sold by his widow in 1887 to the city which required the property for parkland. The only other structures of any consequence were small fishing shacks owned by the Wards, the Strowgers, and the Geddes. The blockhouse at the west end of the peninsula, built by Simcoe in 1793 as a major fortification of his garrison town, had been dismantled in 1815.

In the ensuing years, the Island gained in popularity. With the increasing number of citizens and visitors alike desirous of visiting "Hiawatha," as the Toronto Island was called in the mid to late 1800s, more ferry boats were pressed into service. Most vessels were privately owned and competition, not to mention harbour traffic, was frantic. Following is a list of some of the ferries operating to Wards, Island Park, and Hanlan's Point from the wharves at Church, Yonge, and Brock (Spadina) Streets between 1855 and 1889. This list (Figure 1) is incomplete, as not all vessels operating in passenger service were recorded by the overworked authorities. In fact, in 1887 Mayor Howland requested members of council to prepare a bylaw enabling ferry operations to be turned over to a single company in order to "bring order out of chaos."

As can be imagined, the numerous ferries of all sizes plying Toronto Harbour meant that published sailing schedules were frequently ignored when the weather deteriorated or more lucrative charters became available. By the 1880s, most vessels had come under the control of a handful of owners. Captain John Turner owned the *Luella*, *Sadie*, and *Prowette Beyer*, and Andrew Tymon the *Arlington*, *Jessie McEdwards*, *Kathleen*, *Gertrude*, and *Island Queen*. In 1887, the vessels of Captain Turner's Ferry Company were purchased by the Doty Ferry Company for $14,600. Now, with just two large ferry companies in business, the Doty Ferry Company and Island Park Ferry Company, plus a few individually owned vessels, *Mascotte*, *Muzeppa*, and *Ontario*, the scene was set for the incorporation of a new company which was to eventually monopolize all Island ferry service.

In 1890, the Toronto Ferry Company was incorporated as a joint stock company under financier E.B. Osler as president and Lawrence Solman as general manager. Their first move was to acquire the vessels of the Doty Ferry Company. Two years later the company purchased Tymon's Island Park Ferry Company. The company soon acquired almost all the other vessels in the ferry boat business, giving them a virtual monopoly on hauling the public to and from the Island. In 1895, the Toronto Ferry Company owned the following eleven vessels:

Jessie McEdwards Propeller driven, 15 HP high pressure engine, length 65', width 12'6", weight 12½ tons, capacity 116.

FIGURE 1

Name of Ferry	Date in Service (if known)	Original Owner (if known)	Comments
Fire Fly	1855	Captain R. Moodie	First ferry to offer moonlight cruises on Toronto Bay.
Island Queen	1855		Built in 1843 at Kingston.
Watertown	1864	Captain J. Jackman	Built at Kingston and occasionally ran to the Humber.
Ripple	1864		Advertised as a "miniature steamer with jaunty rig and obliging boy captain."
Princess of Wales	1864	John Walsh	Burnt in 1886.
Bouquet	1866	T. and J. Saulter	Bought in 1868 by Captain Parkinson to run to Parkinson's Hotel at Centre Island.
Ada Alice	1868	Captain J. Goodwin	Purchased by Toronto Ferry Co. in 1901.
Prince Arthur	1868		
Perry	1870	Captain Parkinson	
Transit	1878		
Golden City	1878		
Juliette	1878		
St. Jean Baptiste	1878	John Turner (Turner Ferry Co.)	Built at Quebec; brought to Toronto by Turner, renamed *Sadie* after his wife and sold to Doty Ferry Co. in 1890; rebuilt as double-ender and rechristened *Shamrock* in 1897; burnt in 1907 Bay Street docks fire.
Luella	1880	John Doty (Doty Ferry Co.)	Bought by Toronto Ferry Co. in 1890; carried hundreds on free excursions, especially children to the Lakeside Home at Hanlan's Point; withdrawn from service in 1934, she was to be a museum but was destroyed by vandals; scrapped in 1944.

Name of Ferry	Date in Service (if known)	Original Owner (if known)	Comments
Prowette Beyer		Captain Parkinson	Sold to Turner Ferry Co.
Geneva	1882	Turner Ferry Co.	Operated formerly in Hamilton and Kingston.
Canadian	1882	Turner Ferry Co.	First "double-ender" on Toronto Bay; bought by Toronto Ferry Co. in 1890; renamed *Thistle* in 1897 and burnt intentionally in 1906.
John Hanlan	1884	John Hanlan (Hanlan Ferry Co.)	Built at Port Dalhousie in 1884; ran to Hanlan's Hotel from foot of Bathurst Street; bought by L. Solman and leased to Toronto Ferry Co.
Queen City	1885	Doty Ferry Co.	Launched at the foot of Trinity Street.
Ontario			Destroyed in Esplanade fire of 1884.
Mazeppa			Badly damaged in same fire, rebuilt and later operated on Burlington Bay.
D.C. West		A.J. Tymon (Island Park Ferry Co.)	Renamed *Maud S.*
Mascotte	1886	Island Park Ferry Co.	Built in Toronto and acquired by Toronto Ferry Co.
Arlington		John Murphy	Built in 1878; bought by Island Park Ferry Co. and later acquired by Toronto Ferry Co.
Jessie McEdwards	1876	Island Park Ferry Co.	Built in 1876; acquired by Toronto Ferry Co.
Kathleen	1886	John Murphy	Built in Toronto, bought by Island Park Ferry Co.; acquired by Toronto Ferry Co.
Gertrude	1886	John Murphy	Built in Toronto, bought by Island Park Ferry Co.; acquired by the Toronto Ferry Co.
Island Queen	1889	John Murphy	Built in Hamilton, bought by Island Park Ferry Co; acquired by the Toronto Ferry Co. and burnt at Hanlan's Point, 1918.

Luella	Propeller driven, 24 HP engine, length 66', weight 38 tons, capacity 122.
Canadian	Paddle driven, 120 HP engine, double-ended, double deck, length 122', width 19', weight 230 tons, capacity 340.
Sadie	Paddle driven, 50 HP engine, double deck, length 112', width 35', eight 154 tons, capacity 377.
Kathleen	Propeller driven, 35 HP engine, double deck, length 84', width 18', weight 100 tons, capacity 200.
Gertrude	Propeller driven, double deck, length 75', width 16½', weight 76 tons, capacity 147.
Mascotte	Propeller driven, 15 HP engine, single deck, length 70', width 1', weight 49 tons, capacity 128.
Island Queen	Propeller driven, 15 HP engine, length 73', width 14', weight 23½ tons, capacity 148.

In addition to the preceding, the Toronto Ferry Company acquired two vessels which were under construction for the Doty Ferry Company when ownership changed hands. Both were double-deck, double-end, steam side-paddle vessels, 140 feet long, twenty-eight feet wide, weighing 189.4 tons each and licensed to carry 900 passengers. Each was powered by two twenty-nine horsepower engines. Built by the Doty Engine Company, *Mayflower* was christened by little Jennie Doty on May 24, 1890. One month and four days later, the sister ship *Primrose* slid into the water at the foot of Bathurst Street, following ceremonies climaxed by the traditional breaking of a bottle of champagne over the bow by Miss Mary Williams. Each vessel cost $33,000 to construct and incorporated the latest conveniences and improvements including electric lights. They operated from 7 a.m. to 11 p.m. daily, April through October, until 1938 when they were finally sold for scrap. The eleventh vessel, the *John Hanlan*, was leased by the ferry company and ignominiously put to the torch for the thrill of the public at Sunnyside Beach in 1929.

General Manager and later owner of the Toronto Ferry Company, Lawrence Solman, better known to Torontonians as "Lol," was quite a remarkable man. Born May 14, 1863, he was the son of one of the founders of Toronto's Holy Blossom Temple. In 1885 Solman left Toronto to set up a mail-order business in Detroit. He returned to his hometown and in 1893 married Emily Hanlan, daughter of John and sister of Champion oarsman Ned Hanlan. Lol was very much interested in the development of the Island. He became the general manager of the ferry company and secretary-treasurer of the Toronto Baseball and Amusement Company which ran the International League baseball team, as well as the baseball and lacrosse stadium and amusements at Hanlan's Point. He also became the managing director of the Royal Alexandra Theatre when it opened in 1907, and later managing director of the Arena Gardens on Mutual Street, now known as the Terrace. He also managed Sunnyside Amusement Park for many years. When motion pictures were gaining in popularity in Canada, Marcus Loew, founder of the gigantic Loew's chain of movie houses, made Solman vice-president of the Canadian subsidiary of Loew's Theatres Limited.

Solman was the owner of the Toronto Ferry Company when in 1906 the double-end, double-deck, steam-paddle ferry *Bluebell* — originally spelled *Blue Bell* — was put into service. Four years later Solman officiated at the ceremonies marking the launching of the largest ferry ever to operate on Toronto Bay, *Bluebell*'s sister ship, *Trillium*. Two years after that the company acquired the *Jasmine*, formerly known as the *A.J. Tymon* and the *Ojibway*. By 1926 the citizens of Toronto were anxious to have Solman's ferry fleet come under the control of the municipal government. After considerable negotiating, during which Solman reduced his selling price several times, the city agreed to purchase the fleet of eight vessels for $337,500. The vessels purchased by the city and their dates of construction were: *Luella* (1880), *John Hanlan* (1884), *Mayflower* (1890), *Primrose* (1890), *Jasmine* (1892), *Clark Brothers* (1901), *Bluebell* (1906), and *Trillium* (1910).

The Toronto Ferry Company operated the ferry service for the city from April 1926 until February 1927 when the city transferred the fleet to the Toronto Transportation Commission. Initially the ferries were operated by the Motor Coach Department, but in 1929 a separate Ferry Department was set up by the Commission. In 1928, to replace the *John Hanlan* and the *Jasmine*, the TTC purchased a single-deck twin screw steamer built in 1911, the *T.J. Clark*. While used principally to haul freight, the *Clark* was fitted with firefighting equipment. In 1935 a new steel diesel ferry was built to replace the faithful, but old, *Luella*. Originally christened *Shamrock*, the name was later changed to *William Inglis*. This ferry was named for a well-known Toronto businessman and was constructed for $77,000. Four years later another diesel ferry was put into service to replace the scrapped *Primrose* and *Mayflower*. The *Sam McBride*, named in honour of a former city mayor and long-time Island resident, was built for $150,000 at the Toronto Dry Dock Company. A sister ship to the *Sam McBride*, the *Thomas Rennie*, named for a Toronto Harbour commissioner and businessman, was placed in service in 1951 at a cost of $244,630. In 1956, with the fleet now made up of more modern and efficient vessels, the fifty-year-old *Bluebell* and forty-six-year-old *Trillium* were sold to the Metropolitan Toronto Works Department for conversion to garbage scows.

On January 1, 1962, the entire Island ferry service was transferred from the TTC to the Metropolitan Toronto Parks Department. This department operates the present fleet of ferry boats consisting of the *William Inglis*, *Sam McBride*, *Thomas Rennie*, *Shiawassie* (1962), and *Ongiara* (1963). The flagship of the fleet is the reconstructed 1910 steam, side-paddle *Trillium*.

Peninsula Packet, the second houseboat to operate to the Toronto peninsula, 1843. (*Sir John of the Peninsula* was the first, a decade earlier.) Using the hull of a small Niagara River steamer, Louis Privat, co-owner of the Peninsula (or Privat's) Hotel, built this craft which was powered by two horses walking a treadmill. The ferry was under the command of Louis' brother Peter.

Privat's *Peninsula Packet*, 1849. In 1845 the original vessel was enlarged, given a pointed bow, and a circular treadmill which was propelled by five horses. This craft ran from the Church Street wharf to the hotel wharf until 1850 when it was succeeded by the *Victoria*.

Early Island Ferry Boats

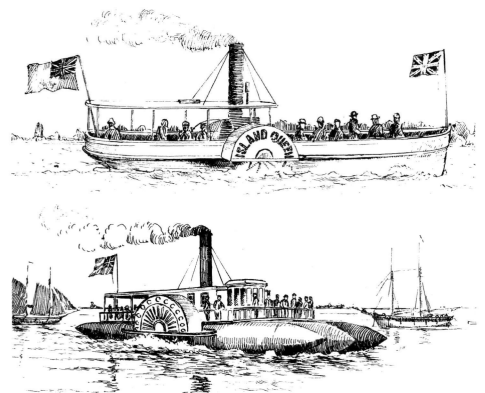

Island Queen, built 1843.

Tinning's Cigar Boat, built 1849, scrapped 1859, and parts used for a bridge over the Don River.

Victoria, built 1850.

Fire Fly, built 1855.

Bouquet, built 1866.

Ada Alice, built 1868.

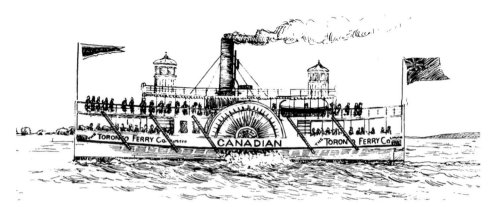

Canadian, built 1882.

Mascotte, built 1886.

Shamrock, renamed 1897. Built in 1878, it was first named *St. Jean Baptiste* and later *Sadie*.

(Top) In 1883 — just eight years after Toronto's now world-famous Hospital for Sick Children opened in a small house near the southeast corner of College Street and Park Lane (now University Avenue) — officials acquired a parcel of land not far from the old lighthouse at the west end of Toronto Island where they constructed a convalescent hospital. Here, thanks to the ongoing benevolence of newspaper publisher John Ross Robertson, children confined to the busy main hospital during the rest of the year could enjoy the soothing amenities afforded by the remoteness of the Island during the summer. Moving the children to and from the ferry docks by horse drawn carriage soon became a Toronto ritual. During the Second World War the Island hospital was used by members of the Norwegian Army Air Force who trained at the Island Airport and lived in a camp called Little Norway at the foot of Bathurst Street.

(Bottom) The Lakeside Home for Little Children.

The *John Hanlan* was built in 1884 at Port Dalhousie, Ontario. Acquired by Lawrence Solman and leased to the Toronto Ferry Company, the *John Hanlan* was turned over to the Toronto Transportation Commission in 1927. On July 19, 1929, the vessel was set afire at Sunnyside to "thrill the crowds" who flocked to the amusement park to watch the "spectacle."

Jasmine was built in Toronto in 1892 and originally known as *A.J. Tymon* after its owner. Rebuilt at Sorel, Quebec, it was renamed *Ojibway* and in 1912, when put into Toronto Island service, was renamed *Jasmine*. In the background, note the clock tower of Toronto City Hall visible through the smoke and haze.

A pair of steam ferries built by the John Doty Engine Company for the Doty Ferry Company in 1890.

Mayflower was a gracefully proportioned double-end steamer and soon became part of the new Toronto Ferry Company fleet. Both the Toronto Ferry Company and the Doty Ferry Company were privately owned. The municipally owned Toronto Transportation (now Transit) Commission took over all Island ferry operations in 1927, and in this view *Mayflower* is seen in TTC livery.

Primrose, *Mayflower*'s sister ship and another product of the Doty Engine Works, was a member of the Doty Ferry Company fleet. She was also launched in 1890 at the Doty shipbuilding yard at the foot of Bathurst Street. In this view, *Primrose* is seen soon after she and *Mayflower* had come under the ownership of the newly organized Toronto Ferry Company. Like *Mayflower*, she too eventually became part of the TTC's Island ferry fleet. Both were scrapped in 1938.

Lawrence "Lol" Solman, general manager of the
Toronto Ferry Company.

Toronto Ferry Company docks. While the
First World War would soon erupt in Europe,
Torontonians by the thousands still found time to
visit the Island. And with the 1914 baseball season
in full swing it was only natural that Hanlan's Point,
where the Toronto team played its home games,
would receive top billing on the destination list,
followed by Island Park at Centre Island and the
cottage colony at Ward's.

Bluebell at the Bay Street wharf, circa 1912. Fresh, bright, and ready for the day's passengers, *Bluebell* waits with the rest of the fleet. *Primrose* and *Mayflower* are moored behind *Bluebell*, and *John Hanlan* and *Jasmine* are at an adjacent wharf. The Lake Ontario passenger steamer *Northumberland* appears in the left background. Note the coal on the wharf which was used to fuel the ferries.

When Edward, the Prince of Wales and the eldest son of the reigning monarch King George V, paid a visit to Toronto in August 1919, among his several duties was to officiate at the cornerstone laying for the Royal Canadian Yacht Club's new clubhouse on Toronto Island. Boarding the RCYC's member launch *Hiawatha* moored at the front entrance of the Toronto Harbour Commission Building, the young Prince quickly arrived at RCYC's specially constructed Island wharf. Here he was met by several hundred Club members and guests who had made their way across Toronto Bay on the ferry *Trillium*.

Trillium had been in service only a few years when an anonymous visitor to the waterfront snapped this undated photograph of the ferry moored near the foot of York Street. Obvious in this view is the provision made in *Trillium*'s early years to allow passenger off-loading from the upper deck. This was necessary to allow the huge number of impatient baseball fans on board the ferry to get off and over to the Island baseball stadium where the best tickets sold on a first come, first served basis.

In keeping with the tradition of naming the larger Toronto Island ferry boats after flowers, TTC officials decided to name the newest addition to its fleet *Shamrock*. The vessel was built in 1935 by the John Inglis Company in a temporary shipyard near the foot of Spadina Avenue, a site that as a result of land filling is now occupied by the King's Landing condominium complex. Shortly before entering regular service, the vessel's name was changed to *William Inglis* to honour the recently deceased president of the John Inglis Company and a prominent city philanthropist and businessman. In this photograph, *William Inglis* has been charted for a private party and decorated as a Mississippi River showboat.

The one thousand passenger Toronto Island ferry *Thomas Rennie* was built in 1950 by the John Inglis Company at a cost of $250,000. She entered regular service in 1951 and was named in honour of Thomas Rennie, a city businessman and member of the Toronto Harbour Commission who had served from 1931 to 1947 and as its chairman since 1938. Rennie died August 4, 1952.

Also built by the John Inglis Company, the *Sam McBride* was launched in 1939. This Island ferry was named in honour of the late Sam McBride who had served on city council for many years. He passed away on November 14, 1936, becoming the first Toronto mayor to die while still in office. "Sam" was also a long-time Toronto Island resident. While the new ferry was ready for service in the summer of 1939, the war delayed the ship's steering gear from being shipped from the English manufacturer. *Sam McBride* was christened by the late mayor's daughter on May 24 of the following year.

Ongiara crossing the Bay, 2006. Research indicates there are two possible origins for the name of this Island ferry, the only vessel in the fleet that is equipped to break ice in the harbour and carry service vehicles. *Ongiara* may come from a First Nation's expression that translates to "point of land cut in two" (a reference to the Niagara peninsula), or from another expression that suggests "the sound of thunder" (the noise made by the cascading waters over Niagara Falls). The $145,000 vessel was built in Owen Sound in 1963 and arrived in Toronto on December 20 after a difficult two-week, 1,290 kilometre trip during which the 24 metre craft was forced to seek shelter from the icy spray numerous times.

For nearly half a century the sound of Trillium's bell was instantly recognized by generations of Toronto Island residents. Soon after the ferry was abandoned in an Island lagoon the bell went missing only to returned, anonymously, once the rehabilitation project got underway.

Life on Ward's, Centre, and Hanlan's Point

Hanlan's Point was often promoted as "Canada's Coney Island," a not too subtle mention to the famous Brooklyn, New York, resort and amusement park. Also seen on this billboard is mention of Island Park, a popular picnic ground at Centre Island.

A survey prepared by John George Howard in 1846 showed that there were but twelve buildings of various sizes and shapes on the entire peninsula, plus a small number of fishermen's shacks near the present Eastern Gap. Twenty-one years later, after the peninsula had been transformed by the 1858 storm, the surveying firm of Wadsworth, Unwin and Brown completed a new survey that showed a similar settlement except that the shacks were missing and a small water pumping station had been set up at the west end of the Island. The significance of this survey was that for the first time the Island had been subdivided, streets laid out and, the city hoped, made ready for settlement. Editorials in the local press, however, described the entire area as anything but a place where one would wish to live. The *Leader* called the Island "a wretched and forlorn looking place," and George Brown's *Globe* of April 30, 1875, admonishes the city fathers thus: "Toronto, in the possession of the Island, has advantages enjoyed by few cities, and it is right her citizens should have the full benefit of them."

Slowly improvements were made, and by the late 1870s there were definite signs that the Island was attracting summer cottagers. At first most of the cottages were built down at the Hanlan's Point end of the Island. To cater to the city dweller who wanted to spend his summer holidays away from the heat of the city, John Hanlan built a twenty-five room hotel at the Point. As filling operations to create more land progressed, it was necessary to move the hotel physically to the west. John was the father of Edward Hanlan, who became world famous as "Ned Hanlan, champion oarsman." Born in 1855, Ned defeated oarsmen from Canada, the United States, Australia, and Great Britain during his rowing career from 1876 to 1880. A grateful city gave him a free lease to property on the Island and his admirers bought him a home worth $20,000.

Down at the other end of the Island, the Royal Canadian Yacht Club built their lovely new clubhouse in 1880 on ten acres of land leased from the city. No one was allowed to purchase their property and even today Islanders continue to lease the land. As the number of summer Island residents began to increase, steps were taken to provide them with a house of worship. Early meetings were held at Hanlan's Hotel and later in George Gooderham's beautiful Island residence to plan the erection of an Anglican Church, and in 1884 St. Andrew's-by-the-lake was consecrated. Built at a cost of $1,400 the church was moved in 1959 from its original location on the lakefront between the lighthouse and Centre Island to its present location further east.

In sharp contrast to the solemn Sunday services being held at St. Andrew's-on-the-Lake, an amusement park, with its noisy barkers, hurdy-gurdy merry-go-round, and unique vaudeville acts, began to draw crowds to the Island. Folklore has it that about 1885 J.C. Connor, a former manager of the old Royal Theatre on King Street East, obtained permission from John Hanlan to operate amusements in a small park beside the hotel. Naturally, as the Island became more and more popular, so too did the amusement park. Soon it became necessary to move some of the cottages at the Point to allow expansion of the park. Some years later, in 1897, a baseball and lacrosse stadium was built and soon the International League

Toronto Maple Leaf baseball team moved their home games to this stadium from Sunlight Park, east of the Don River on Queen Street. They continued to play and win pennants at the Island Stadium until owner Lol Solman moved the team to his new stadium at the foot of Bathurst Street in 1926. Here the team played until 1967 when they folded after eighty-one years of professional ball.

About the same time as the amusement park opened at Hanlan's, the Lakeside Home for Children was established on the Island through the generosity of *Evening Telegram* publisher John Ross Robertson. This institution provided handicapped children from Toronto with a summer of fresh air and sunshine. Thousands of kids were given a special summer at the home from the time it opened in 1883 until 1928 when the Thistletown Hospital opened northwest of the city. The Lakeside Home structures were used to house war veterans for many years thereafter. The recuperative powers of a visit to the Island prompted the Toronto Street Railway Company to propose in 1886 a streetcar line from King and Yonge Streets, along King, down Bathurst, across the Western Gap on a swing bridge to Hanlan's Point and along the south shore to Ward's. As the use of horses as motive power was impractical on such a long route, it was proposed that the line be operated by steam or electric vehicles. The idea was revived by the Toronto Incandescent Light Company five years later, and although the streetcars never materialized, electric lights soon did.

In 1890, the Toronto Ferry Company was formed and within a few years all Island-goers were travelling aboard vessels owned by this company.

The education of Island children has always been an important concern. Mrs. Durnan, the wife of the third light keeper, turned her own small house into a school and began teaching the children of the local fishermen. Later, in 1888, a one-room school was built and was used until it was destroyed by fire in 1905. A larger, two-room school opened the following year. To serve a growing younger generation, the school expanded several times. Then, in 1960, the Toronto Board of Education established the Island Natural Science School. Originally, students in grade five and six from city schools would come to the island for one week, living in the school's residence. Students were taught programs designed to give them an appreciation and greater knowledge of nature. On February 1, 1999, both the Island Natural Science School and the Island Public School (the latter continues to look after the educational needs of the Island children) moved into a new building on Centre Island. The new building is a modern facility and incorporates the Island's natural environment into its structure, both inside and out. Currently, students in grade five and six from the inner core of the City of Toronto visit the Island Natural Science School. Programs continue to focus on giving students experiences which allow interaction with and appreciation for nature, while incorporating Ministry of Education curriculum.

The 1890s saw major increases both in the Island's physical size and in its population. In fact, the population became sufficiently large to warrant the formation of an Island Residents Association to deal with all municipal matters relating to the Island. By 1895, the Island Supply Company was established to provide the residents with, as the newspaper ad reads, "high class groceries, fancy fruits, nuts, bread and other necessities … at very reasonable rates." The company had two outlets, one at the former Clarke residence on Centre Island and another at Hanlan's Point. On August 3, 1900, the three thousand summer residents organized a volunteer fire brigade and soon there were three fire stations, each equipped with a fire reel and lengths of hose. While the amenities of city life were being provided, the city was also busy increasing the size of the Island by filling lagoons with dredging from the harbour bottom and barge-loads of excavated earth from the expanding St. Lawrence Market on the mainland. The area of the Island had, by the early 1900s, nearly tripled to 563 acres. The volunteer fire brigade was given its first major test on September 10, 1903, when fire erupted inside the six-year-old wooden grandstand at Hanlan's Point. Within two hours the entire structure and adjacent bleachers were a smoldering ruin. A new and more modern grandstand was quickly constructed, but it too was destroyed in an even more serious fire that broke out August 10, 1909. This conflagration not only destroyed the athletic facilities but also Hanlan's Hotel, the "Figure Eight" roller coaster, the "Dip the Dips" ride, the Gem Theatre, the Penny Arcade, the Amusement Hall and School of Fun, the restaurant, and the shooting gallery. Losses totaled more than $200,000 and tragically the cashier of the theatre was killed in the inferno. A new expanded playground soon grew from the ashes, and under the direction of Lol Solman the Leafs were playing baseball in a grander grandstand the following year. The old merry-go-round survived only to be demolished for no apparent reason.

In 1911 major changes were made to the city's water supply system. As a result of a break in the old water supply pipe under Toronto Bay, Torontonians had been supplied with polluted bay water and, although no serious illness resulted, it was obvious the city had to improve the system. The old filtration plant on the Island, in operation for more than fifty years, was taken out of service and a revolutionary new plant was erected north of the old. This new filtration plant was put under the direction of Norman Howard, who soon became the Island's unofficial doctor and who, according to his son Alan, "made more than 8,000 medical calls without fee." The plant was enlarged in 1916 and by 1977 was capable of pumping up to 120 million gallons daily of clear, cold water to the citizens.

While the amusement park and small summer cottages developed at Hanlan's, and the Gooderhams, Nordheimers, and other wealthy Torontonians built their palatial retreats at Centre Island, the quiet solitude of Ward's Island was attracting a different type of visitor. By the early 1910s, campers had discovered the pleasures of Ward's and the area was dotted by hundreds of canvas tents. Soon wooden additions were constructed and eventually these additions became the main residence.

In 1913, to improve access to the Island, a tunnel was proposed under the new Western Gap which had been relocated further south and opened in 1911. No actual construction was started at that time, but in 1935 excavation for this tunnel was started. For some reason, however, work stopped almost immediately thereafter. Every so often the idea surfaces again, but the diggings of 1935 are still the closest the federal government has come to building the tunnel.

A decision made by the City Council on July 9, 1937, was to have a far-reaching effect on the future of Toronto Island. The Port George VI Airport, to use its official title (it was renamed Billy Bishop Toronto City Airport in 2010), opened in 1939 as an integral link in transcontinental commercial air service and was to be a municipal air terminal as well as connecting the city with Ottawa, Montreal, Buffalo, Cleveland, Detroit, and Chicago. The development of the airport required the removal of existing cottages and demolition of the amusement park and ball stadium. Some of the cottages were "floated" to the opposite end of the Island in an operation directed by a descendant of David Ward, an early settler who gave his name to the eastern part of the peninsula. Frank Ward remembers floating at least thirty cottages from Hanlan's to Algonquin Island, where some remain to this day.

The establishment of the airport and the resulting disappearance of the amusement park and stadium, combined with the opening of the new Sunnyside Amusement Park on the mainland in 1922 plus the growing popularity of the automobile, all led to an increasing neglect of the Island by city dwellers. Then came the war, and without their cars (gasoline and tires being rationed) people began day-tripping to the Island in such great numbers that soon the TTC's entire fleet of ferries was hard-pressed to carry the millions of war-weary passengers to the Island. Then, because of the housing shortage that followed the war, that number was supplemented by the more than eight thousand summer residents, among which were almost two thousand who lived there year round.

What did the Islanders and their guests do for amusement? They sipped sodas at Ginn's Casino, snacked at Bill Sutherland's Manitou Hotel, danced to Eddie Stroud's band, bicycled, canoed, rode the merry-go-round, or just strolled from Ward's to Hanlan's and back again. And, of course, there was the ferry boat ride complete with nerve-shattering whistle which drove youngsters and oldsters alike to cover their sunburned ears with sunburned hands.

Soon the newly incorporated Municipality of Metropolitan Toronto became the new landlord and the Metro Parks Department got on with the job of converting Toronto Island into a park as ordered. Demolition of the massive mansions and frail cottages began in the late 1960s and today permanent residents are found only on Ward's and Algonquin Islands.

PROGRAMME of Band Concerts and Other Attractions:

At Hanlan's Point for the Season 1897

A two-hour Band Concert every evening and Saturday afternoon (weather permitting) by one of Toronto's celebrated Military Bands.

Grand Bicycle Races every Saturday evening by the fastest Canadian and American riders.

Eastern League Baseball

TORONTO at Home with

Springf'ld, June	12	Springf'ld, July	27	Buffalo, August	17
Springfield "	14	Springfield "	28	Buffalo "	19
Springfield "	15	Springfield "	29	Buffalo "	20
Rochester "	21	Scranton "	30	Springf'ld, Sept.	7
*Rochester "	22	Scranton "	31	Springfield "	8
Rochester "	23	Scranton Aug.	2	Springfield "	9
Syracuse "	24	Wilkesbarre "	3	Wilkesbarre "	10
Syracuse "	25	Wilkesbarre "	4	Wilkesbarre "	11
Syracuse "	26	Wilkesbarre "	5	Wilkesbarre "	13
Buffalo a.m. July	1	Rochester "	6	Scranton "	14
Buffalo, p.m. "	1	Rochester "	7	Scranton "	15
Buffalo "	2	Rochester "	9	Scranton "	16
Buffalo "	3	Syracuse "	10	Providence "	17
Providence "	23	Syracuse "	11	Providence "	18
Providence "	24	Syracuse "	12	Providence "	20
Providence "	26	Buffalo, August	16		

*Two Games in afternoon at one price of admission.

Games called at 4 p.m. excepting Saturdays and Holidays, 3.30 p.m. Morning Games 10.30 a.m.

SAT., JUNE 19—Lacrosse Match—La Nationale (Montreal) vs. Tecumseh.

SAT. JULY 17—Lacrosse Match—Quebec vs. Tecumseh. Other Lacrosse Matches being arranged

WED. AUG. 18—Toronto Police Amateur Athletic Association Games.

Roof Garden Every Evening—Rain or Shine—at 8.15,

10c.—ADMISSION—10c.

Reserved Seats, 15c.   Children 5c. and 10c.
Change of Artists Every Week

Continuous Performances RICH & RAMSAY Managers

This Programme Subject to change

THE Toronto Ferry Co.

LIMITED

TIME TABLE
For Season 1897

Steamers leave from the WEST SIDE of YONGE ST SLIP and from Brock St. Wharf.

The Company reserves the right of altering this Time Table.

BRANCH OFFICE	W. A. ESSON,
YONGE ST. WHARF	MANAGER
TEL. 2965	HANLAN'S POINT

Island Telephone, Hanlan's Point

An 1897 timetable for the Toronto Ferry Company. This was the first season baseball was played on the Island and the Leafs had strong competition from many American teams. If baseball or lacrosse wasn't their thing, Island revelers could enjoy a night of vaudeville at the Roof Garden. Reserved seats were only fifteen cents.

In this undated photo, mothers and their infants
enjoy some relief away from the steamy-hot city
thanks to the generosity of Toronto Ferry Company
manager Lawrence Solman who frequently provided
free rides on board one of his Island ferries.

In addition, Sir William Mackenzie, president of the Toronto Railway Company, offered free rides on his streetcars for any child who wished to learn to swim. These "free bathing cars" would roam predetermined routes along which children would wait with bathing suit and towel at hand to be taken to and from several supervised bathing stations. One of these facilities was located at the Western Sandbar, an area that's now the site of the Billy Bishop Toronto City Airport.

CHILDREN
LEARN TO SWIM

Supervised Swimming Stations are maintained by the City at **SUNNYSIDE, WESTERN SAND BAR, FISHERMAN'S ISLAND,** and on the **DON,** above Winchester Street.

Street Cars are provided daily by the Toronto Railway Company to carry children to these stations.

ALL FREE OF CHARGE

TIME-TABLE OF FREE STREET CARS

Bay Street crossing, 1913. Early in the 1900s the Toronto Ferry Company moved to new docks on newly reclaimed land near the foot of Bay Street. Pedestrians, however, still faced a long walk from the streetcars on Front Street and an almost equally dangerous crossing of the railway tracks (now in this view protected by barriers). Note the constable assisting the crowds and the watering cart keeping down the dust.

Bay Street docks, July 1, 1907. Because of the huge crowds that made their way to the ferry docks on the busy public holidays such as Victoria Day, Dominion (now Canada) Day, and Labour (now Simcoe) Day, it was often expedient to load the ferry *Bluebell* from the front, the side, and by means of a special gangway leading to the upper deck. Soon after *Bluebell* entered service in 1906, special gates were installed on the upper deck to keep the crowd from rushing to the bow as the ferry approached the Hanlan's Point dock. Before these so-called "cattle gates" were installed the extra weight up front would cause the stern to rise out of the water. This resulted in the rudder having little or no effect as *Bluebell* fishtailed its way towards the dock. To help alleviate the worsening overcrowded and unsafe conditions on the existing ferries in 1909, the Toronto Ferry Company decided to add a virtual clone of *Bluebell* to the fleet and they would name her *Trillium*. In the background of this photo is the popular passenger lake boat *Turbinia* preparing to depart for Hamilton.

Island ferry docks, 1927. As the configuration of Toronto's waterfront changed due to land filling operations by the Toronto Harbour Commission, the location of the Island ferry docks changed, too. In this view they are situated between Bay and York Streets on the newly constructed Queen's Quay. Note the ex-Toronto Railway Company wooden streetcar as it waits for passengers on the newly established Toronto Transportation Commission service to the docks. In the background are three of the ferry boats that were turned over to the Commission when the city gave it the mandate to operate the Island ferry service.

Island ferry docks, 1931. Four years have passed since the previous photograph was taken. The TTC's modern new Peter Witt streetcars now connect the ferry docks with the city north of the railway viaduct. Queen's Quay has been paved and across the street the former (and often very muddy) parking area has been turned into new parkland called Bayside Park. At the extreme right of the view we see a portion of the newly constructed Terminal Warehouse, originally a utilitarian cold storage facility that was beautifully restored and given a new life in 1983. It is now known as Queen's Quay Terminal.

Hanlan's Hotel, circa 1900. Built in 1880, this was the second hotel operated on the Island by a member of the Hanlan family. Several years earlier John Hanlan had a small hotel and in 1880 his son Edward, known better as Ned, built this magnificent structure at Hanlan's Point. In later years the hotel was operated by James Mackie, who called Hanlan's Point "the Coney Island of Canada." The hotel burned to the ground in a devastating fire in August 1909 that saw one person killed and most of the adjacent amusement park and sports stadium destroyed.

Edward "Ned" Hanlan. Born in Toronto in 1855, Ned moved to the Island as a boy when his father went into the hotel business. He soon developed tremendous skill at rowing and at the age of just 18 defeated Sam Williams to become the city's single-scull champion. By 1876 Ned was the champion of Ontario. Later that year he entered a competition at the Centennial Exhibition in Philadelphia and set a new world record on the three-mile course. Hanlan continued to race and win awards in Canada, the United States, and England until he was eventually defeated by William Beach on Parramatta River in Sydney, Australia, in 1884. Although Hanlan lost the race, a summer resort town just north of Sydney was renamed Toronto in honour of one of Canada's greatest sportsmen. Ned also served two terms as a Toronto alderman. He died on January 4, 1908.

(Top) Hanlan's Point Amusement Park, 1912. Thousands flocked to the amusement park at Hanlan's Point to ride the "Dip the Dips," the "Figure Eight" roller coaster, or to watch "Hamburg's Big Spectacular Water Show," in which Madge Macdonald performed her celebrated disrobing act while in the water. The large merry-go-round in the left background withstood the flames that destroyed most of the amusement park in the summer of 1909.

(Bottom) One of the most popular turn-of-the-twentieth century attractions at Hanlan's Point was an unusual feature known as "J.W. Gorman's Diving Horses." The two steeds, *King* and *Queen*, would climb a long, sloping ramp and, on cue, dive into the adjacent lagoon. Attempting this same performance today those poor horses would plummet into the Island airport runway.

Baseball and lacrosse were popular spectator sports at Hanlan's Point Stadium. The first Island stadium, a wooden structure, was destroyed by fire in 1903. A second wooden stadium was soon erected, but it, too, was destroyed in a major conflagration that broke out on August 10, 1909. A new concrete stadium was constructed the following year and it was home to the Toronto Maple Leaf baseball team of the International AAA League (one step below the majors) until 1926 when the team moved to a new stadium over on the mainland that had been built on reclaimed land at the foot of Bathurst Street by the Toronto Harbour Commission.

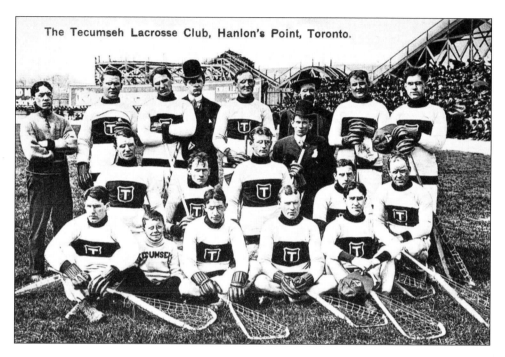

The Tecumseh Lacrosse Club, Hanlon's Point, Toronto.

The "Dodgem" cars and merry-go-round were just two of the many rides at Hanlan's Point amusement park. After Sunnyside amusement park on the mainland opened in 1922 business at Hanlan's decreased sharply, although these visitors don't seem to have noticed. However, by the mid-1930s the bubble had finally burst and the Island amusement park closed for good.

This undated aerial photograph shows the Hanlan's Point amusement park sometime after the second wooden stadium, which had burned in August 1909, had been replaced by a modern 18,000 seat concrete version. Also visible is the park's mammoth "switchback railway" (roller coaster). The body of water west of the stadium would eventually be filled in to expand the parkland at Hanlan's Point. To the left of centre in the photo the newly constructed Western Channel has been completed while nearby work continues on converting the swampy areas of Hanlan's Point into dry land on which a new airport would be constructed. Now known as Billy Bishop Toronto City Airport, the field opened in 1939 as the Port George VI Airport, a name selected to honour the reigning Monarch who visited Canada that same year. The long row of buildings along the edge of Toronto Bay are those of a shipyard where lake freighters were being constructed and where minesweepers would be built for the Royal Navy and the Royal Canadian Navy during the Second World War.

Maple Leaf Stadium, 1933. In 1926 a mammoth new baseball stadium, which would quickly become known as the "Fleet Street Flats" (Lake Shore Boulevard was initially known as Fleet Street), was built at a cost of $750,000 at the foot of Bathurst Street by the Toronto Harbour Commission. It would come to be regarded as the finest facility in the minor leagues. In the background is the Hanlan's Point Stadium, which was demolished several years after this photograph was taken to make way for expanded parkland, as well as a new Island airport, a twin of the one that would be built northwest of the city near the Village of Malton. The Tip Top Tailors clothing factory is now the Tip Top Lofts condominium. At the lower left is the Rogers Majestic factory where radios, complete with Edward Rogers' revolutionary AC vacuum tubes, were manufactured. A condominium now occupies the site.

The "Main Drag" on Centre Island, 1910. Flanked by numerous small stores, Manitou Road was Centre Island's main street. This Valentine & Son postcard view looks south from the cast iron bridge (which is still there) over Long Pond and towards the lake. Edward English's boathouse is to the left and next door is Art Sainsbury's confectionary shop. Some of the Centre Island residents who would frequent the shops (more likely they would send a servant) were stockbroker Stuart Playfair, barrister T.C. Robinette, investment broker Arthur Massey, city engineer Charles Rust, and Gordon Gooderham, president of Gooderham and Worts.

The three-man crew (Engineer E. Newall, Captain G.M. Brown, and Mate H. Reynolds) of the Toronto Island ferry *Luella*, 1929. *Luella* was one of the most popular vessels in the entire fleet. She was built in 1880 at Walter Armour's small shipyard on the water's edge at the foot of Simcoe Street. The ferry's unusual name resulted when Armour combined his daughter's first name, Lulu, with that of his wife Lella. Powered by a one-cylinder engine, *Luella* plied the waters of Toronto Bay for more than fifty years until she was retired from service following the end of the 1934 season. After a summer or two as a beached relic she was summarily scrapped.

Ad from the *Ward's Island Weekly*, August 2, 1919.

Cottages at Ward's Island, 1911. While day-trippers took in the rides and games at Hanlan's Point and the rich threw another log on the fire to help ward off the cool summer evening breezes drifting through their Centre Island "mansions," campers were pitching tents at Ward's Island. Travelling salesman Arthur Etwell, tailor Malcolm McBain, store clerk George Sockett, and Massey Hall employee Norman Withrow were four of the many who erected tents at Ward's where they and members of their families could seek relief not too far away from the steamy city. In some cases, remnants of those tents and boxes they came in formed the starting point for some of the more permanent structures that began to appear across this part of the Island. After years of bickering over whether people should be allowed to live on Ward's Island or whether it should be parkland, today more than 600 people live in the 262 residences located on both Ward's and Algonquin Islands.

While Centre Island was the location of many large summer homes belonging to Toronto's rich and famous — as well as a popular public picnic area known as Island Park — and Hanlan's Point was the site of a large amusement park and sports stadium, Ward's Island, on the other hand, was the exclusive domain of those with only a day or weekend to spend away from the city. In this circa 1910 penny postcard view, some of the boys have pitched a tent and erected a shack ready to rough it at Kamp Kanibuls.

A favourite pastime for visitors to Toronto Island was to watch the various vessels, large and small, come and go through the Eastern Channel. In this undated photograph, two fashion conscious spectators watch as the *S.S. City of Ottawa*, a passenger and package freight steamer, departs Toronto Harbour preceded by the tug *D.W. Crow*. In the background, *S.S. Chicora*, a former American Civil War blockade runner that was subsequently converted to a passenger vessel and saw 36 years of service on the Toronto–Niagara River route, makes for her city berth. While the photograph is undated, the fact that the *City of Ottawa* was a frequent visitor to the Port of Toronto between 1906 and 1913 under the Merchants Montreal Line flag helps define a period of time the photo could have been taken. Thanks to Jay Bascom for helping identify the ships in this photograph.

Trillium Today

Work on the vessel's new steel and aluminum superstructure was well underway when on September 17, 1975, a member of Herb Fraser and Associates staff hooked a steam line to the ship's whistle and *Trillium* announced she was alive once again. (Photo by Gordon Champion)

On November 7, 1975, and after more than a year in the hands of the experts at Herb Fraser's Port Colborne, Ontario, shipyard, *Trillium* awaits permission from the St. Lawrence Seaway Authority to enter the Welland Canal and begin her return to her home port across Lake Ontario. Waiting to assist are the tugs *G.W. Rogers* and *Bagotville*. (Photo by Mike Filey)

More than thirty years after transiting the Welland Canal for the first time back in 1975, *Trillium* again makes her way back to Toronto through the historic waterway on May 12, 2006. This voyage follows a government-mandated, five-year ship inspection at the same Fraser shipyard. (Photo by Yarmila Filey)

Philip Troyer took these two photographs of *Trillium* as the historic craft departed Centre Island on her way to the City Dock at the foot of Bay Street in the summer of 2008.

While touring Canada, Andy Burgess, a visitor from England, paid a visit to Toronto's waterfront, where he captured this intriguing photograph of two of the city's most historic ships — the paddle steamer *Trillium* and the tall ship *Empire Sandy*. The latter was launched near Newcastle-Upon-Tyne, England, in the summer of 1943 and originally served as an "Englishman/Larch Class" deep sea salvage tug and spent the rest of the war assisting disabled Royal Navy warships on the North Atlantic, Mediterranean Sea, and Indian Ocean. In 1950 she arrived in Canada, and for the next twenty years she towed logs and barges on Lake Superior before being sold for scrap. Days before its demise, the hard-working vessel was purchased, and over a period of years rebuilt in the style of an 1800s three-masted schooner. Since the early 1980s, *Empire Sandy* has earned her living as a charter vessel on Toronto Bay.

Another fascinating photograph by Philip Troyer. This one captures a trio of Toronto landmarks in one view, the historic 1910 Toronto Island ferry *Trillium*, the CN Tower that opened to the public in the summer of 1976, and at the extreme right the seventy-two-storey First Canadian Place, the tallest building in Canada.

Prior to the rehabilitation project being undertaken, it was determined that the type of lifeboat *Trillium* originally carried was no longer acceptable by modern government standards. In an effort to retain the vessel's historic 1910 "look," two replicas of the original lifeboat were manufactured out of fiberglass using moulds of one of the original lifeboats. (Photo by Mike Filey)

The Polson Iron Works

Polson Iron Works Limited
═══════════════════Toronto═══════════════════

Steel Shipbuilders
Engineers and
Boilermakers

Steel Steamers, Tugs and Dredges
(Hydraulic and Dipper type)

Engines Marine (simple, compound and triple), Stationary, Brown Automatic and Corliss, Slide Valve, Vertical and Hoisting.

Boilers Heine Patent Water Tube for stationary purposes, Thorneycroft - Marshall for marine use, Horizontal Tubular, Marine of all styles.

Write us for Estimates
before ordering

Tanks Smoke-stacks and Sheet Iron Work.

Works and Office : Esplanade East, Foot of Frederick and Sherbourne Streets **Toronto, Ont.**

This advertisement for Polson Iron Works Limited appeared in a 1908 trade magazine and shows the extent of the manufacturing operations carried out at the company's factory on the water's edge at the foot of Sherbourne Street.

During the mid-1800s many classy schooners and formidable steamboats were built on the shore of Toronto Bay. One of the largest shipbuilding yards was that of the Polson Iron Works Company. Established in 1833 by William Polson, the Toronto yard of this company was located at the foot of Sherbourne Street on the Esplanade. Following the destruction of the CPR steamer *Algoma* on Lake Superior, Polson's opened a new yard in Owen Sound in 1888 and commenced construction of a replacement vessel to be known as *Manitoba*. This 305-foot vessel was the first steel ship to be built in Canada and was the largest vessel on fresh water. Initially only small craft were built at the Toronto yard, most of the work consisting of the manufacture of large engines and boilers which were shipped by rail to the Owen Sound yard. Soon it became profitable to construct larger vessels at the Toronto location as well, and the proper facilities were constructed by expanding the plant to cover the waterfront between Sherbourne and Frederick Streets.

In 1905, with a payroll of 450, the company was awarded a contract to construct a new Island ferry for the Toronto Ferry Company. It was to be 150 feet in length with a thirty-foot beam and powered by an inclined compound steam engine connected to side paddles. The *Bluebell* was launched on April 12, 1906, and was one of the most modern ferries on the Great Lakes. Four years later, a sister ship, christened *Trillium*, took to the water.

In 1912, the Polson Company built the seventy-one-foot launch *Kwasind* for the Royal Canadian Yacht Club and three years after that launched the largest vessel of any kind seen to that time on Lake Ontario, *Ontario #2*. It was built for the Grand Trunk Railway and was put into service hauling loaded coal cars from Charlotte, New York, to Cobourg, Ontario. During the Great War the Polson plant built a large number of ocean-going freighters. Towards the end of the war the *War Temiskaming*, *War Algoma*, *War Hamilton*, and *War Halton*, each 261-foot freighters, were launched at the foot of Sherbourne Street. The last vessel was the 150th ship to be built by Polson Iron Works.

The end of the war also brought an end to orders for new ships and in an attempt to keep their more than one thousand workers employed, Polson negotiated a contract with the Norwegian government to build ten "salties." The Canadian government first approved the arrangement but subsequently rejected the plan just as the contract was to be signed. Tragically, on March 11, 1919, the Polson Iron Works Company filed for bankruptcy. Within a year the company had vanished from the business world. In the late 1920s the new Toronto railway viaduct was constructed burying beneath it any trace of the once powerful enterprise. One of the finest vessels to come from their shipyard, *Trillium* remains as a tribute to the craftsmen of Polson's.

Franklin Bates Polson (1858–1907). Established in Toronto in 1883 by Frank and his father William, the Polson Iron Works Company became one of the largest shipbuilding concerns in the country. In 1888, following the destruction of the steamer *Algoma* on Lake Superior, Polson's established a branch plant in Owen Sound where the CPR steamer *Manitoba* was built. For many decades the *Manitoba* was the most elegant vessel on the Great Lakes. Over the years Polson's built more than 150 vessels including the *Bluebell* in 1906 and *Trillium* in 1910. The company faced bankruptcy in 1919 following the First World War and vanished from the Toronto business world soon thereafter.

Polson Iron Works, 1914. It was here that the Toronto Ferry Company's new Island passenger vessel *Trillium* was built and subsequently launched on the afternoon of June 18, 1910. The factory's approximate location relative to today's street plan would be south of The Esplanade between Sherbourne and Frederick Streets. Eventually this once busy industrial site was buried beneath the cross-waterfront railway viaduct that was constructed in the late 1920s. To the extreme right of the view are the rusted remains of the *Roller Boat*, a creation of Prescott, Ontario, lawyer and inventor Frederick Knapp that was also a product of the Polson shipyard. Its unusual tubular shape was to revolutionize shipping as it literally rolled over the waves. It didn't.

Polson Street in the city's Port Lands District
recognizes the Polson Iron Works as one of
Toronto's most important waterfront industries
of the late 1800s to early 1900s.

Rebirth of the *Trillium*

The special day, June 18, 1910. The Toronto Ferry Company's new steam ferry boat was launched at the Polson Iron Works yard. After much uncertainty regarding a name for the new vessel (among the rejected possibilities were *Arbutus*, *Hawthorne*, and *Golden Rod*, all names of flowers), the name *Trillium* was selected. The idea of naming the larger Island ferries after plant life was a tradition carried on by Lol Solman's Toronto Ferry Company, with *Trillium* joining *Mayflower*, *Primrose*, and *Bluebell* already in service. As seen in this newspaper photograph, the new craft obviously required considerable additional work after the launching to get her ready to enter regular service. Amazingly, just two weeks later *Trillium* was ready for the happy crowds eager to visit the amusement park and baseball stadium at Hanlan's Point on the Dominion Day weekend. In 1910, the cost of building *Trillium* amounted to $75,000. Restoration of the vessel in the mid-1970s was slightly in excess of $1 million.

Saturday, June 18, 1910, dawned clear and warm, but the morning edition of the *Toronto World* predicted afternoon thundershowers. Theodore Roosevelt's triumphant return to the States from his tour through the African jungle was the feature item on the front page. Less prominently displayed was a report that 300 unionized plumbers in Toronto were set to strike for more money. Meanwhile in Montreal, employees of the Grand Trunk and Canadian Pacific Railways had almost reached an agreement with their bosses on a new settlement. In another item, it was reported that an Indiana pilot had set a new altitude record of 4,503 feet in his Wright biplane. Closer to home, Vicar-General McCann was preparing to officiate the next day at the cornerstone-laying ceremonies at the new $80,000 Lady of Lourdes Church on Sherbourne Street. On the sports page, the *World* was predicting a win for the second place Eastern League Maple Leaf baseball team against Providence later that day in Rhode Island. A small ad on the page advised fans that the game would be shown on the Paragon Scoreboard at Massey Hall. The real estate page informed the reader that eighty building lots in the Eglinton-Yonge area were selling for $8 to $12 a foot frontage, "but hurry, they're going fast." Down on Walker Avenue someone was selling his eight-room house for $4,200, while a nine-room dwelling in the Annex was going for $300 more.

According to an ad on the entertainment pages at Solman's place on Hanlan's Point, "the Marvel of the Age M. Holden" was going to dive 150 feet into a pool of ice-cold water and later "Darling's Dog and Pony Circus" would perform while the Body Guard Band played on.

And hidden on page 16 was a short item reporting the successful launching of a new ferry boat for the Toronto Ferry Company.

It had been a busy morning for eight-year-old Phyllis Osler, the granddaughter of Edmund Osler, president of the ferry company. She and her mother were ready when the black Cadillac arrived at their Rosedale Avenue home to take them to the shipyard where Phyllis would christen the new ferry. A sister ship to the *Bluebell*, *Trillium* took to the water just after noon. Almost immediately the workers were busily installing the cumbersome Scotch boiler and finishing off the remainder of the wooden superstructure. By July 1, a mere twelve days after the launching, the ferry company's flagship began the first of her forty-six seasons carrying hundreds of thousands of pleasure seekers safely across Toronto Bay.

In 1926, *Trillium*, along with seven other vessels of Solman's ferry fleet, was purchased by the city. The following year saw a new owner's name painted on the fore and aft bulwark of *Trillium* — Toronto Transportation Commission. It seemed somewhat incongruous that she was part of an equipment roster that included streetcars, buses, and by 1954, subway cars. In 1956, *Trillium* was made ready for another season of service, but she was never used: the more modern ferries were equal to the task of carrying a declining number of Island visitors. On July 25, 1957, Metro Toronto Works Department paid $4,200 to the TTC for the vessel. They planned to convert it to a garbage scow by stripping off the superstructure and removing the engines as they had done a year earlier with *Bluebell*. But suddenly, on September 17, because of some fortuitous change in plans, *Trillium* was towed to an Island lagoon near the old lighthouse where she remained for sixteen years. Twice — in 1962 and again in 1963 — cursory investigations were made into the possibility of restoring *Trillium* to service. The 1962 survey was extremely negative, while in1963 the project was declared possible at an estimated cost of $250,000. The latter report was not acted upon. Perhaps the timing wasn't right.

In the years following *Trillium*'s "final trip," thousands of Island visitors watched as the once proud flagship of the ferry fleet deteriorated into an almost unrecognizable pile of firewood. Even the tour boat guides commented on the sad derelict as they passed by. Occasionally a visitor expressed his concern that nothing was being done to halt *Trillium*'s continuing decline.

In 1973, on one of our frequent trips to the Island, my wife and I voiced a similar concern, and when we next met our friend, then City of Toronto Alderman Art Eggleton, we discussed with him the possibilities of undertaking a restoration. Art spoke to Metro Parks Commissioner Tommy Thompson whose department controlled the ferry operations, and soon a meeting

of persons interested in seeing the historic old vessel reactivated was convened by the Toronto Historical Board. This preliminary meeting was attended by Commissioner Thompson; Works Commissioner Ross Clark, whose department had legal title to the vessel; Ed Barnett, architect and member of the Toronto Historical Board; Alan Howard, well-known Toronto marine historian and curator of the Marine Museum; Brigadier-General John McGinnis, managing director of the THB; and myself. In order to determine whether the vessel could, in fact, be returned to operation, Mr. Champion was requested to carry out an initial feasibility study. This request was approved by Metro Council on April 23, 1973. The subsequent report was extremely positive in its conclusions regarding the rehabilitation of *Trillium*, and on November 13, 1973, persuaded perhaps by the enthusiasm of Messrs. Godfrey, Eggleton, and Thompson, the Metropolitan Toronto Council approved the $950,000 project of reactivating the ferry under the direct supervision of Gordon Champion. The rebirth of the old sidewheeler was underway. The following pages document the various stages of the rehabilitation program which culminated in *Trillium*'s triumphal return home on November 7, 1975.

Boat landing at Hanlan's Point, Toronto

Hanlan's Point dock, August 16, 1913. In this picture postcard view, *Trillium* is seen unloading passengers at the amusement park dock. Because of their size and carrying capacity, both *Trillium* and her twin *Bluebell* were regularly used to carry the large crowds attending the popular amusement park and 18,000 seat baseball stadium at Hanlan's Point. While both vessels were licensed to carry a maximum of one thousand passengers, it was said that on the busiest days there were so many on board one would have to breathe alternately with one's fellow passenger. Note the large merry-go-round in the left background. Oh, and count the hats, an early type of sunscreen.

September 7, 1958. In 1957 *Trillium*, now of no further use, was removed from service and put to one side until officials could determine what to do with her. At one point there were plans to strip the vessel down to the hull which would then be used as a scow as had happened to her sister *Bluebell*. When the latter turned over in a gale any plans to repeat the idea were scrubbed. Time went by and eventually *Trillium* was towed across the bay to a lagoon near the Island school and left to rot. This unique photo was supplied by Bruce Baker, whose father operated the Toronto Island taxi service and happened to photograph *Trillium* as she was under tow to what everyone thought would be her final resting place.

September 6, 1972. The remains of two once proud and popular vessels continue to wait the end in a quiet Island lagoon. In the foreground is a hull, all that remains of what was the Island ferry *Bluebell*. Years later the hull was taken to the southernmost part of the 5-kilometer long Leslie Street Spit where it was unceremoniously discarded, thereby becoming part of this unique public urban wilderness.

Bluebell being torn apart in the Keating Channel, 1957. When it became obvious to city officials that the passenger capacity of the three more modern diesel-powered ferry boats — *William Inglis*, *Sam McBride*, and *Thomas Rennie* — was more than sufficient to handle the dwindling Island-bound crowds it was decided to scrap the older boats: *Bluebell* first, then *Trillium*. In this photograph the older vessel (*Bluebell*, by four years) has been stripped of her wooden (and rotted) superstructure leaving the twin paddlewheels, the engine, and the controls visible. Soon only the riveted steel hull would be left. Except for a fortunate twist of fate, *Trillium* would have been next.

The summer sun and winter sleet and snow had not
been kind to *Trillium*'s wooden superstructure as
the abandoned vessel awaited the end in a secluded
Island lagoon. By the time this photo was taken in
mid-1973, all her original brass fittings had vanished.

December 7, 1973. On this date, following a decision by Metropolitan Toronto Council to perform initial feasibility studies in order to determine whether restoration was practical, *Trillium* was towed to the Metro Works marine yard at the foot of John Street. At the wheel of the Metropolitan Toronto Works Department tug *Ned Hanlan II* is Sid Farmer who, along with Captain Dallas Milne, kept a close watch on *Trillium* during those many years she languished in the lagoon.

December 7, 1973. An "old" Toronto landmark
poses with a partially completed "new" city landmark.

May 16, 1974. The job of removing the rotted superstructure was awarded to McNamara Marine in Whitby, just east of Toronto. In this view *Trillium* is almost completely shorn of its entire wooden superstructure as it rests naked in the company's dry dock.

June 29, 1974. Project engineer Gordon Champion inspects the hull of *Trillium*. Initial inspection of *Trillium*'s hull had taken place during the cold winter months at the Metropolitan Toronto Works slip at the foot of John Street. This had been followed by a more detailed inspection while *Trillium* was high and dry in the McNamara dry dock in Whitby. The most important thing found at this stage of the inspection process was the lack of serious pitting of the ferry's 64-year-old riveted steel hull. Serious pitting could have occurred over the 56 years the vessel had operated on Toronto Bay plus another 15 years sitting in the relatively clean water of the Island lagoon. It wasn't until this fact was confirmed that the project to return *Trillium* to operating condition (rather than to simply a static display artifact) could, in fact, proceed.

July 15, 1974. Back home again, though quite literally a mere shadow of her former self, *Trillium* is towed to the Keating Channel to await the outcome of contract negotiations prior to embarking on the next phase of the project. Note the CN Tower and the Toronto Hilton Harbour Castle Hotel (now the Westin Harbour Castle Hotel) under construction in the background. The latter opened in 1975, the former one year later.

October 1, 1974. Once Metropolitan Toronto officials had selected the Port Colborne, Ontario, firm of Herb Fraser and Associates to carry out the major restoration work the next step was to get *Trillium* there. Towed across Lake Ontario and through seven of the eight locks of the 43.5 kilometre long Welland Canal by the tug *G.W. Rogers*, this photograph shows *Trillium* and her friend gingerly making their way through Lock 2. *Trillium* and the tug would meet again in another 13 months.

October 3, 1974. As soon as *Trillium* arrived at
Ramey's Bend (on the Canal in Port Colborne) Herb
Fraser's people began stripping off the old, decayed
wooden decking and paddlewheel casings. The
five people most involved in the rehabilitation are
captured in this photograph. They are (left to right):
Bunny MacLean, Gordon Champion, Alex Morris
(in dark hat), Fred Weaver, and Ken Parkes. Here the
gentlemen inspect *Trillium*'s main engine crossheads.

Trillium's open engine room, 2008. This photograph is quite a contrast with the one on the preceding page. The 2008 view shows the results of the lengthy and meticulous restoration of *Trillium*'s open engine room. A couple of passengers watch as ship's engineer Victor Pavlenko puts *Trillium* through her paces.

A close-up view of the starboard side-paddle and floats, November 1, 1974. An in-depth inspection of this photograph shows the deteriorated oak floats and a mechanism known as a Jenny-nettle — a system of rods and levers that permits each float to enter the water vertically, thereby reducing the power lost if the float were fixed to the frame cross member and forced to enter the water at an oblique angle. It was necessary to disassemble this mechanism, clean and renew all pins and bushings, and install new wooden floats. Note the large shaft at the centre left of the view. It connects with the main engine.

Trillium's double compound steam engine as it looked before restoration. *Trillium's* steam engine works like this: Steam generated by the boiler is fed to the high pressure cylinder seen on the right of the photograph. The steam forces the piston and its connecting rod to turn the large crankshaft, which in turn causes the paddlewheels to rotate. Because *Trillium's* crankshaft is one piece, both paddle wheels always turn in the same direction. The partially used steam is then fed to the adjacent low pressure cylinder where additional thrust is obtained. The fully expanded steam is then directed to the ship's condenser where it is changed back to water for reuse in the boiler. In the photograph the cylinder covers of the seventeen-inch high-pressure and thirty-four-inch low-pressure cylinders have been removed to permit inspection of the cylinder bores. Even after many thousands of hours under steam, the cylinder walls showed amazingly little wear thanks, in part, to the competence of the engine room crews of past years.

In this photograph project engineer Gordon
Champion performs some preliminary testing
to determine *Trillium*'s "heeling" characteristics.
Heeling is the tendency to lean to one side during
manoeuvers. The large concrete weight sitting on a
wheeled dolly can be moved into various positions
to simulate external pressures on the vessel.

Trillium's original Scotch marine boiler sits behind her new automatic boiler. While much work continued during the long, cold winter of 1974–75, one of the most important events was the arrival of *Trillium*'s new oil-fired automatic boiler. This boiler is rated at 10,000 pounds of steam per hour at a pressure of 165 psig (pound-force per square inch gauge) and replaced the original coal-fired, hand-stoked Scotch marine boiler. As the bottom photo reveals, when it came time to install the new unit precision measuring certainly paid off.

February 19, 1975. Here the new steel decking, bulwarks, and side-paddle casings have been installed. Inside the hut, Bunny, Ken, and Alex are busy refurbishing the main engine components while below deck, pumps and valves from the recently scrapped lake tankers *Texaco Brave* and *Cardinal* are being installed. In order to retain as much authenticity as possible, all replacement equipment had to be of the same time period as *Trillium*'s original equipment.

June 23, 1975. The third phase of the rehabilitation program was the erection of the aluminum superstructure and related features. This contract was awarded to Dominion Aluminum Fabricating Limited of Mississauga, Ontario. In this view the first aluminum beams and pillars are being put into place. These sections form the promenade deck and supports for the top or shade deck. Note that *Trillium* now has a new funnel, an exact replica of the badly corroded original stack.

September 16, 1975. *Trillium*'s new aluminum
superstructure is complete.

October 1, 1975. In this view painters have already applied special etching and primers and now give *Trillium* a coat of white marine paint. The main and prom decks have been covered with a special "Neotex" floor coating and the passenger control gates are in position. Note the ventilators at the base of the funnel and the loading ramp supports at the bow. Replicas of the ship's original lifeboats and radial davits have been positioned on the port and starboard side of the upper deck. Because the federal government decreed that this type of safety equipment can no longer be used (lifeboats have been superseded by flotation devices), and in order to keep to keep the "lines" of the vessel, it was necessary to have fiberglass replicas manufactured by craftsmen in Georgetown, Ontario.

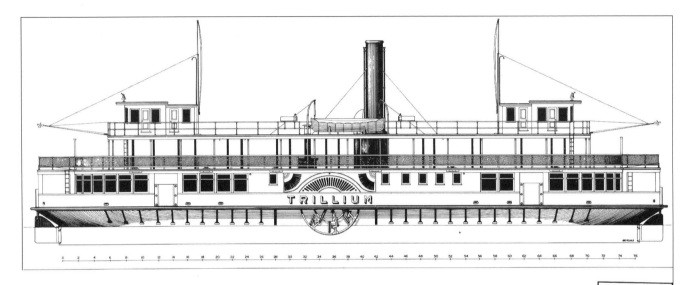

SIDE PADDLE WHEEL
FERRY BOAT

TRILLIUM
SIDE
ELEVATION

BUILT BY
POLSON IRON WORKS LIMITED
TORONTO 1910

SHIPS LEADING DIMENSIONS
Length......
Between Perpendiculars
.....137'-4"
Extreme Breadth   47'-0"
Moulded Breadth   30'-0"
Depth Moulded   9'-6"
Registry No.   126833
Registered Tonnage 463·42
Nominal HP   48·1
Indicated HP   350
SCALE
FEET

REHABILITATION CARRIED OUT
DURING 1974/5. BY THE
METROPOLITAN PARKS DEPT
OF THE MUNICIPALITY
OF METROPOLITAN TORONTO

PROJECT CONSULTANTS
& ENGINEERS
D.G. CHAMPION ENGINEERING LTD

These precise illustrations of *Trillium*'s engine room and side elevation were created from original Polson Iron Works plans supplied by Robert Campbell. Other original plans from Campbell's collection were invaluable in aiding in the rehabilitation program.

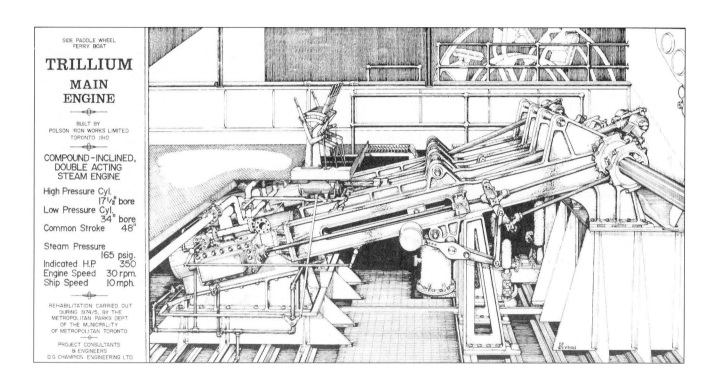

October 22, 1975. Of special importance was the unique decoration over the paddlewheels. In the top photo, Martin Kovac precisely positions masking tape to ensure an accurate reproduction of the 1910 embellishments on the paddle-boxes. The final shading of the letters was added just prior to the vessel's return to Toronto. Note one of the two cast aluminum beaver inserts over the name.

October 25, 1975. In his downtown Toronto workshop, Vern Barton and his assistant Sam Santoro prepare the wood trimming that would cover the numerous modern aluminum pillars throughout *Trillium*. The two craftsmen lovingly duplicated all of the vessel's original, but deteriorated, wood trimmings, railings, and doors. In fact, even the wooden benches were meticulously constructed to look, and more importantly *feel*, exactly like the original.

With her many small incandescent lights gleaming, *Trillium* nears completion. The masts and navigation lights are in place as are the two fibreglass lifeboats created as duplicates of the original wooden lifeboats. The radar has been installed and tested and the fore and aft bells, cast from a mould of an original *Trillium* bell, sit atop the wheelhouses. The spear poles, usually used to assist in docking manoeuvres, have also been installed. Painted on the fore and aft port and starboard bulwarks is the name of *Trillium*'s original owner, the Toronto Ferry Company.

November 7, 1975. Departing Port Colborne at 9:00 p.m. on November 7, 1975, *Trillium*, towed by the Canadian Dredge and Dock tugs *G.W. Rogers* (left) and *Bagotville*, glides silently and smoothly across Lake Ontario on her way home. This photo was taken about 6:00 a.m. the following morning and shows the tugs lashed together and under the command of one captain while the other captain rests after a busy night descending seven locks of the Welland Canal.

It was shortly after noon on June 18, 1910, when the official
launching party gathered at the Polson Iron Works yard
at the foot of Sherbourne Street. Members of the party
included (extreme left) Lawrence "Lol" Solman, the Toronto
Ferry Company's general manager, and (in front) Osler's
granddaughter Phyllis Osler.

On June 18, 1976, exactly sixty-six years after
Trillium's launching at the Polson yard, the same
Phyllis Osler (Phyllis Aitken at the time) unveils
a special commemorative plaque at an event that
recognized the historic vessel's return to service.

Twenty years after being retired from active service *Trillium*
returned to Toronto Bay on May 19, 1976, for a special charter
cruise. In this photograph she is given a spectacular welcome
by the Toronto Fire Department's fireboat *William Lyon
Mackenzie*. In command of *Trillium* that historic evening was
the late Captain Richard Farley with engineer Eric Carter at
the controls. For the next few hours *Trillium* paddled about
Toronto Bay while three hundred guests sang and danced
to the music of the York Lions Steel Drum Band. *Trillium*,
flagship of the Metropolitan Toronto Parks Department ferry
fleet, will be used for private charters during the week and
public cruises of the harbour on weekends.

Illustration Credits

Barb and Win Boyd: pages 67, 83

Bruce Baker: page 84

City of Toronto Archives: pages 36, 38, 58, 77

Gordon Champion: pages 93–94

Metro Toronto Reference Library/Toronto Public Library: pages 20, 27–30, 33, 59

Mike Filey: pages 5, 14, 31–32, 34 (bottom), 39–44, 46, 51–57, 61 (bottom), 62–63, 65–66, 69–72, 74, 76, 78, 80, 85–92, 95–114

Toronto Transit Commission Archives: pages 34 (top), 35, 64, 68

Toronto Harbour Commission Archives/Toronto Port Authority Archives: pages 37, 60, 61 (top)

Other Books by Mike Filey

Toronto
The Way We Were
978-1-55002-842-3
$45.00

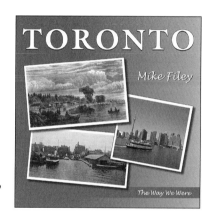

Mike Filey serves up the best of his meditations on everything from the
Royal York Hotel to the devastation of city disasters such as Hurricane
Hazel and the Great Fire of 1904, and spins yarns about doughnut shops
old and new, milk deliveries by horse, swimming at Lake Ontario's beaches,
Sunday blue laws, and how both world wars affected Torontonians.

Toronto Sketches 9
"The Way We Were" Columns from the Toronto Sunday Sun
978-1-55002-613-9
$19.99

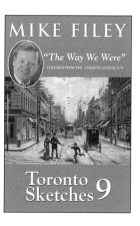

Mike Filey's column, "The Way We Were," first appeared in the *Toronto Sunday Sun*
not long after the first edition of the paper hit the newsstands and front porches on
September 16, 1973. Since that day more than three decades ago, Mike's column
has enjoyed an uninterrupted stretch as one of the paper's most popular features.
This ninth volume features a variety of stories, including a look at the birth of Rex
Heslop's Rexdale community and a few fascinating tales about the city's streetcars.

A Toronto Album 2
More Glimpses of the City That Was
978-1-55002-393-0
$24.99

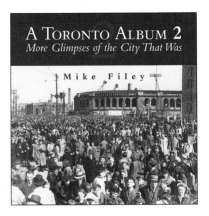

A Toronto Album 2 is a photographic journey through bustling Toronto from the late 1930s to the early 1970s. Among the 100-plus photographs is a quartet that shows the remarkable changes to Toronto's skyline over a half-century. Others capture the 1939 royal visit and glimpses of a few landmark buildings we weren't smart enough to keep. This is a keepsake Torontonians will treasure.

Available at your favourite bookseller.

DUNDURN PRESS
www.dundurn.com

What did you think of this book?
Visit www.dundurn.com for reviews, videos, updates, and more!

Marquis Book Printing Inc.

Québec, Canada
2010